THE OBSCURED PRINCIPLES UNVEILED

The Hidden Laws That Govern the Seen and Unseen

1

This book was written with devotion, silence, and sacred remembering by one who walked the path from fragmentation to wholeness, from forgetting to embodiment. May it meet you where the soul never lied.

Table of Contents

Introduction

The Forbidden Flame

You did not find this book by accident.

There are books that call to the curious.
There are books that inspire the seeker.
And then there are books like this—
Books that **summon** the remembering.

Not with sound, but with *recognition.*
A silent chord within you begins to hum.
A language you were never taught, yet rises in your throat like breath.
A path whose dust already clings to your bones—because you have walked it, in lifetimes or dreams.
This is not discovery. It is remembrance.

This is not a book.
It is a **threshold.**
The ash-marked door carved into the inner sanctum of your soul.
And now, standing before it, *you remember.*

Once, long ago, there were those who walked between the worlds—
priests and priestesses of the Hidden Flame,
guardians of a wisdom too potent for the unprepared.
They did not speak it. They **encoded** it—
in myth, in symbol,
in the silence between hieroglyphs.

They knew:
Truth must be veiled to protect both the truth and the unready.

So the Principles were obscured.
Whispered from mouth to ear,
sealed in temples with no doors,
preserved beneath layers of time and forgetting.

But forgetting is never final.

For thousands of years, these laws were veiled—
not out of fear. Not out of greed.
But out of **reverence.**

Reverence for timing.
Reverence for readiness.
Reverence for the sacred itself.

There was a time when the world moved in rhythm with the divine.
When temples breathed alongside the Nile,
when stars dictated festivals,
when names held power,
and silence was holy.

But the fall came—not of empires, but of memory.
The sacred was scattered—
coded into myth,
buried beneath dogma,
guarded in symbols the world forgot how to read.

Yet nothing sacred is ever truly lost.
Only sealed… until the moment of return.

That moment is now.

We live in an age of false light and quick revelations,
of hollow words dressed in gold.
But beneath the noise, a deeper current stirs—

a call not to awaken,
but to **remember**.

You are not reading this because you are curious.
You are reading this because **you are called.**
You carry a matching code.
A resonance long dormant, now **reigniting.**

These are not ideas.
They are **laws.**
Not man-made, but cosmos-born.

They govern the **Seen** and the **Unseen.**
They operate whether you believe or deny.
And when you align with them,
reality **bends toward clarity.**

But take heed:
This path is not one of passive learning.
This is the **Path of Embodiment.**

To read is not enough.
You must *live* each law.
Speak it. Move it.
Etch it into your days through **ritual, breath, and fire.**

Within these pages live nine ancient principles—
Each a gate. Each a flame.
Each waiting for your hand upon the handle.

This is the **return** of what was sealed.
The lifting of veils.
The reopening of temple doors.
The remembering of the *Obscure Principles.*

So pause now.
Place your hand upon your heart.
Close your eyes.
And whisper:

"I remember."

You are not reading a book.
You are stepping into a temple.

Let us begin.

1. The Principle of Dual Vision (Udjat)

Sacred Insight

He who sees only with the eyes is blind to half the world.

There is a way of seeing that pierces veil and shadow.
A sight not bound by light, but born from within it.
It is not taught—it is *unsealed.*
And those who walk the path of the Obscure must learn this first:

There are two eyes.
One for the world that lies before you.
One for the world that lies within.

To walk the path of the Obscure is to stand at the threshold between worlds—
not only the spiritual and the material,
but the **Seen and the Unseen.**

This division is not a flaw. It is a **design.**
What you see is the echo.
What you *sense* is the source.

The Seen is what is shaped: form, result, movement.
The Unseen is what shapes it: thought, energy, symbol, vibration.

Every reality is born twice—first in the Unseen, then in the Seen.
To live unaware of this is to stumble through illusion.
To awaken to it is to become *a participant in the shaping.*

The ancients knew this truth and gave it a name: **Udjat**—
the Eye of Horus.
Whole.
Healed.
Awake.

To see with both eyes is not merely to observe—it is to *know*.
To read the symbols beneath circumstance,
to decode the patterns in people, dreams, delays, and desires.
To behold not just what a thing is,
but what it *means*.

Those who see only with the outer eye
are tossed by appearances, trapped in surface truths.
But the initiate of Dual Vision is no longer deceived.
She sees the physical *and* the energetic.
The moment *and* the myth.
The visible *and* the current pulsing beneath it all.

This principle does not ask you to reject the visible world.
It asks you to *complete it*.
To add the dimension that was forgotten—
the felt, the intuitive, the symbolic, the sacred.

He who sees only with the eyes is blind to half the world.
But she who sees with both
**is no longer ruled by appearances—she becomes the one who
deciphers them.**

Practical Teaching

Awakening Symbolic Sight and Inner Perception

Before the initiate is given the sacred lens,
she must first awaken the **impulse to look deeper.**

Symbolic sight is the inner capacity to perceive meaning within form—
not as metaphor, but as a *truth more real than appearance.*
This is the first practice: to **refuse surface seeing** as the whole.

The world around you is not random.
It is not mute.
It is **a field of mirrors, metaphors, messages.**
A living script, shaped by energy, intention, memory, and resonance.
You are not just *in* the world—you are *in conversation* with it.

Everything that appears in your life is a **glyph.**
Every delay, every encounter, every pattern is a **message encoded in form.**
Symbol is the native language of the Unseen.

To awaken symbolic sight is to begin **decoding that conversation.**

It starts with a shift in question.
Do not ask:

"What is this?"

Ask instead:

"What is this showing me?"
"What is this pointing toward beneath the surface?"

This is the art of **decoding the present.**

- A conflict may be revealing a buried belief.

- A repeated frustration may be the echo of an unhealed wound.

- A seemingly small coincidence may be a nudge from your deeper knowing.

This is not superstition. It is **symbolic literacy.**

And as you learn to read your life in this way,
your perception becomes power.
You begin to choose not only *how* you see,
but *how you respond,*
and in doing so—**you begin to shape.**

Because perception is the **first gate of manifestation.**
You cannot shape what you do not perceive.
And you cannot transform what you do not first **name.**

To see clearly is to reclaim your place as **co-creator of your reality.**

The Udjat: Sacred Lens of Awareness

The Udjat—often called the Eye of Horus—is more than a symbol.
It is a *living architecture of perception.*
A sacred map of sight restored, of awareness made whole.

In the ancient temples, it represented **healing after fragmentation.**
The myth tells us Horus lost his eye in battle with Set—
a battle between chaos and clarity, shadow and sovereignty.

The gods restored his eye piece by piece,
and what returned was not merely sight—
it was **sacred vision**, made stronger through wounding,
and holy through reassembly.

To work with the Udjat is to reclaim your right to see clearly—
not just outwardly, but inwardly, symbolically, energetically.

The Eye is not a passive witness.
It is a **lens**—a conscious filter that reveals layers:

- what is happening

- what it *means*

- what it reflects in you

- what it is here to transform.

When you invoke the Udjat in daily life,
you are not invoking an image.
You are invoking a *state of being.*
One who sees through time, symbol, energy, and cause—not just effect.

The shape of the Udjat itself is a code:
a spiral of intuition, a slash of logic, a brow of memory,
a drop of breath, and a curve of vision.

It is a reminder:

Vision is wholeness.

To see with sacred awareness is to see the pattern, not just the moment.

To view the world through the Udjat is to adopt a lens
that seeks meaning—not just appearances.
It is to see not only with your eyes,
but with your memory, your intuition, your knowing.

In the temples of Kemet, the Udjat was used as a **calibration**—
a way to align perception with truth.
To see rightly was considered a sacred act—
because how you see determines what you create.

Each stroke, each curve, represented a faculty of perception:
sight, hearing, thought, breath, intention, and feeling.

When unified, these created **true vision**.
Not passive. Not reactive.
But conscious, symbolic, and *creative*.

To look through the Udjat is to ask:
What pattern is unfolding beneath this moment?
What is unseen, but still shaping what I see?
What wholeness is waiting to be restored in my perception?

The initiate of Dual Vision trains herself to return to this lens—
not just in ritual,
but in *every interaction, every interpretation, every decision.*

She knows: **how you see is how you shape.**

How Surface-Level Seeing Blocks Inner Transformation

To the untrained eye, all things appear as they are.
But to the initiated eye, no thing is ever *just* what it seems.

The surface is the mask.
The transformation lies beneath.

Most people remain bound not by circumstance,
but by their **interpretation** of circumstance.
They confuse what is *visible* with what is *true*.

They say, "This is happening to me."
But they never ask,
"What is this revealing in me?"

This is the veil of surface-seeing:
where emotion clouds truth,
where reactivity replaces reflection,
where appearance becomes a trap.

Surface seeing reduces experience to flatness:

- A breakup becomes only loss—not rebirth.

- A delay becomes only frustration—not divine redirection.

- A challenge becomes only a problem—not a portal.

When you stay at the surface, you are ruled by external forms.
You react. You spiral. You fragment.
You lose the power to interpret—and thus, the power to *reshape*.

But when you train the inner eye,
you begin to **respond instead of react.**
You ask:
"What pattern is this revealing?"
"What lesson have I summoned by my own vibration?"
"What truth is trying to reach me beneath this appearance?"

This shift is not philosophical. It is alchemical.
Because transformation does not begin with action.
It begins with **perception.**

You cannot alchemize what you haven't recognized.
And you cannot recognize what you refuse to see beyond the surface.

This is why Dual Vision is the First Principle.
Because transformation begins not in doing,
but in *seeing differently.*

The one who sees the Unseen
unlocks the power to reshape the Seen.

Ritual: Opening the Eye

A Rite to Awaken Symbolic Sight and Charge the Sacred Tools

Purpose:
To awaken the inner eye, call in the restored vision of the Udjat, and activate the gesture and mantra that will serve as daily tools of perception and power.

The Heart of the Ritual

Before you begin, know this:

The power of this ritual lies not in the candle, not in the words, but in the **feeling** you bring to it.
The ancient temples were built not with stones alone, but with *intention, reverence, and clarity of will.*

So bring that to this moment.

Even if you whisper, whisper with your whole being.
Even if you sit for just five minutes, sit as if *your inner world is listening.*
Because it is.

What You Will Need

- A candle (white, indigo, or gold)

- A quiet space

- Your breath, your voice, your hands

- Optional: a symbol of the Eye of Horus

1. Light the Flame

In silence, light the candle.
Let the act be slow, reverent.
Speak:

**"I call the Eye that sees the Seen and the Unseen.
I light the fire that does not burn, but reveals."**

Let the flame steady. Gaze with soft focus.

You are not just lighting wax.
You are **activating perception.**
You are saying: *"Let the unseen become visible within me."*

---

2. Call the Eye by Name

Bring two fingers to your **brow point**—the center of inner vision.

Close your eyes.

Speak slowly, with depth:

**"Udjat.
Whole.
Healed.
Awake.
Open now within me."**

Let the sensation of *seeing inwardly* rise.
Feel the veil thin.
This is not imagination—it is *remembrance.*

---

3. Charge the Gesture

Keep your fingers at the brow.
Inhale and exhale three times through the gesture.

Know this: **from this moment forward, this gesture is activated.**
You have charged it through attention.
It is now a **signal to your deeper self**: "See through the illusion.
Return to truth."

This is not a tool for performance. It is for *power*.
It will respond to the **state** you hold when you use it.

---

4. Speak the Mantra Into Power

Still holding the gesture, speak with clear tone:

"I see with both eyes."

Again, with breath and presence:

"I see with both eyes."

And once more, with full intention:

"I see with both eyes."

Let the words become more than language.
Let them become **permission.**

---

5. Seal the Tools

Place both palms over your heart.

Whisper:

"Let what has been seen never be unseen."

Blow out the flame gently.
You are not extinguishing it—you are **carrying it inward.**

Embodiment Key

The Principle of Dual Vision (Udjat)

These are the sacred tools you now carry forward:

Mantra:

"I see with both eyes."
This mantra reconnects you to symbolic sight.
Use it to dissolve confusion, reactivate clarity, and align with the truth beneath appearances.

It is most powerful when:

- You are emotionally triggered or overwhelmed

- You sense something is off but can't name it

- You are making an important decision and want deeper clarity

- You feel lost in the noise of surface-level reality

- You're tempted to judge a person, situation, or outcome at face value

This mantra cuts through illusion.
It calls the inner eye to open.
It shifts you from reaction to reflection—
from confusion to *symbolic command.*

Gesture:

Two fingers placed at the brow point (between the eyebrows)
This is a signal to your body, mind, and energy field:
"I am choosing to see."

It is best used:

- In real time when you feel scattered, overwhelmed, or reactive

- In private moments of recalibration—before sleep, before prayer, before speaking

- Before entering a space that may carry heavy energy or illusion

- When something triggers you and you want to **respond,** not react

The gesture brings the energy of the mantra **into the body.**
It connects thought to action.
It reorients your focus without needing words.

Anchor Use:

Repeat the mantra silently. Touch the brow gently. Breathe.
Even in public. Even mid-conversation.
This is your return point.

It tells your nervous system: **"We are seeing deeper now."**

These tools are not made of matter. They are made of **meaning.**
And meaning is fed by *use.*

Each time you use the gesture—**with presence**—you charge it.
Each time you speak the mantra—**with intention**—you deepen its resonance.

Over time, they become more than a technique.
They become a **signature of your awareness.**
A symbol your body recognizes. A signal your energy obeys.

They grow in power because **you do.**

2. The Law of Sacred Order (Ma'at)

Sacred Insight

All that is flows in rhythm—divine chaos obeys hidden balance.

Before creation, there was not silence.
There was rhythm.
There was **Ma'at**.

She is not goddess as persona—she is **Law incarnate.**
The pulse behind planets.
The symmetry in snowflakes.
The truth that underlies all becoming.

Ma'at is not man-made order.
She is not the structure of control, but the *harmony of alignment.*
She is the law that governs both galaxies and grief—
not by command, but by resonance.

The ancients depicted her with a **feather upon her head,**
because truth must be light.
The heart, at death, was weighed against it—
not to punish,
but to reveal.

Were you aligned?
Did your words match your soul?
Did your actions move in rhythm with what is sacred?

This is the Law of Sacred Order:
That **all things, even chaos, move within a greater pattern.**

Storms cleanse.
Death renews.
Disruption rebalances.

Even the things you fear are working toward wholeness—
but only when you attune to the deeper rhythm.

To invoke Ma'at is not to demand control.
It is to become *available* to harmony.

Order is not rigidity.
It is the music of alignment.
It is a life where your inner truth and outer expression are
matched.
Where your spirit, mind, and body move as *one current.*

This is not a moral law. It is a **cosmic one.**
It governs stars and breath.
It governs relationships, manifestation, and memory.

You cannot escape Ma'at.
You can only live out of sync with her—and suffer.
Or align with her—and thrive.

To live in Sacred Order is to become a vessel for clarity, peace, and
flow.
To break from it is to spin in confusion, exhaustion, and resistance.

So the question is not,
"What is happening to me?"
But:
"Where am I out of rhythm with truth?"

Ma'at does not judge.
She simply reveals.

And once revealed, you may return.

Practical Teaching

Micro vs. Macro Imbalance

Small misalignments become great disruptions.

Imbalance does not always arrive with thunder.
More often, it begins as a whisper.
A small "yes" when you meant "no."
A skipped meal. A restless sleep.
A moment of pretending to be okay.

These are **micro misalignments**—
small, daily fractures in your inner order.

One skipped truth becomes a distorted relationship.
One ignored need becomes chronic exhaustion.
One misaligned choice becomes a life path that no longer fits.

Over time, these micro fractures multiply.
They shift your center.
They bend your path.
And when they accumulate beyond a threshold—
the macro imbalance is summoned.

That's when life sends the signal louder:

- A relationship ends suddenly, but it had been straining for months.

- The body breaks down after years of ignoring the fatigue.

- A crisis erupts, seemingly out of nowhere—but it was *building.*
  That is not punishment. It is *correction.*

26

The initiate of Ma'at learns to read the small signs **before** the storm:

- Feeling chronically rushed or scattered

- Saying yes out of fear, guilt, or habit

- Being productive but not peaceful

- Numbing instead of facing

- Inner resistance that doesn't go away

These are not failures.
They are **invitations**—to return to rhythm.

Ask yourself:

- **Where am I out of sync with myself?**

- **What truth am I avoiding?**

- **What am I sacrificing in the name of keeping things together?**

Ma'at teaches this law:
The **macro always mirrors the micro.**
If you ignore the whisper, the shout will come.

But if you attune to the whisper—
you realign before the world must correct you.

Practice of Sacred Noticing:
Take one day. Watch for every moment you feel a subtle internal "no."
Each time, pause. Breathe. Ask:
"What would bring me back into alignment right now?"
A truthful word? A boundary? A moment of rest?

This is how micro misalignments are healed—
not with drama, but with **honest, daily return.**

Spiritual Chaos as Misalignment, Not Punishment

Life does not punish. It rebalances.

There is an ancient misunderstanding, still alive in many hearts:
that when life becomes chaotic—
when things fall apart, break down, go silent or dark—
it must be a sign of **spiritual failure.**
That you did something wrong. That you're not aligned enough.
That the divine is displeased.

This is not the voice of Ma'at.
It is the echo of fear.

Ma'at does not punish.
She **reveals.**
She does not create suffering to judge you.
She allows **imbalance to become visible** so that you may return.

Chaos is not cruelty. It is correction.
Not in the form of wrath, but in the form of *invitation.*

When you drift too far from your center,
your life will reflect it—not to shame you,
but to call you **back into alignment.**

A blocked path may mean you've outgrown it.
A sudden shift may be the only way the soul could get your
attention.
An inner breakdown may be a forced release of something false.

If you resist, you suffer.
If you listen, you recalibrate.

This is Sacred Order:
That even disruption is part of rhythm—
if you **interpret it with clarity.**

So the initiate of Ma'at stops asking,

"Why is this happening *to* me?"
And instead asks,
"Where did I leave myself?"
"What truth have I ignored?"
"Where am I out of rhythm with what I know?"

This is not self-blame.
This is self-authority.

There is no shame in having wandered.
Only power in **remembering how to return.**

Practice of Response Over Reaction

Next time life feels chaotic—before trying to fix it—pause.
Ask:

- What rhythm did I stop listening to?

- Where did I override my body, my boundary, my knowing?

- If this were a message, not a punishment, what would it be saying?

Even in chaos, there is order trying to reassert itself.
And if you respond with awareness,
you become the balancing force.

Restoring Balance to Shape Reality from Clarity

You do not shape reality by force. You shape it through inner coherence.

When your life is in chaos, you do not need more effort.
You need **order.**

Not control. Not perfection.
But Sacred Order—the inner state where your mind, body, soul,
and speech are moving as one current.

From that place, something ancient begins to happen:
Reality shifts.

The ancients did not use the word *manifestation.*
They spoke of **bringing the inner into balance so the outer may
reflect it.**
They knew: the world is not separate from your field.
It responds to your **state.**

When you are in alignment, life begins to respond with clarity.
Not always ease—but *meaning, movement, flow.*

This is the hidden power of Ma'at:
She is not just the law of balance.
She is the **womb of resonance.**
When your internal world is in harmony, the outer world begins to
mirror it.

What does alignment look like?

Alignment is not about always feeling good.
It is about **being true.**

- When your body says no, you honor it

- When your intuition speaks, you listen

- When your energy is low, you rest instead of forcing

- When you feel afraid, you pause instead of performing

Each act of inner truth returns you to Ma'at.

From that state, your desires gain gravity.
Your presence becomes magnetic.
Your actions carry weight—not because they are big,
but because they are **aligned.**

Practice: Return Before You Act

A moment of stillness that restores sacred alignment.

Before you speak.
Before you commit.
Before you post, decide, text, reach out, or walk away—pause.

This is the moment Ma'at begins.

You are not stopping to delay.
You are stopping to **realign.**
Because how you act while out of rhythm shapes what you create—
and what you must later correct.

Ask yourself:

- **Am I acting from center, or from fear?**

- **Am I trying to force something into order—or am I returning to it?**

- **Is there a small truth I've been avoiding that would shift this completely?**

These moments may be subtle:

- You're about to say yes to something that exhausts you

- You're replying to a message with pressure in your chest

- You feel urgency, tightness, or fog before a choice

Each one is a **door.**
Not to control, but to **correction.**

In that pause, breathe.
Close your eyes. Feel your body. Ask:

"What would bring me back into harmony right now?"
Not the perfect choice. Not the right answer. Just the truer rhythm.
It may be a breath.
A boundary.
A delay.
A different word.

This is the act of walking in Ma'at.

It is not loud. It is not dramatic.
It is the quiet, powerful choice to move from alignment—
again and again.

And when you do, the outer world begins to trust your field.
The chaos softens.
The path reorders.
And life, once again, begins to respond in rhythm.

Ritual: Weighing the Heart

A rite to restore inner balance and return to sacred rhythm.

Purpose:
To realign your inner state with Ma'at—
through breath, truth, and stillness.
This ritual does not fix. It **reveals.**
It is not a performance. It is a return.

You will need:

- A quiet space

- A comfortable seat

- Your hands

- Your willingness to be honest

(Optional: Have a feather nearby—real or symbolic. It will remind the body of what the heart is being weighed against.)

---

1. Center the Body

Sit with your back straight.
Close your eyes.
Let your breath deepen—not to control it, but to **meet it.**

Inhale.
Exhale slowly.
Three rounds.

Feel your body as it is.
Heavy or light.

Tense or open.
Welcome it all without judgment.

---

2. Place the Hands

Place one hand on your **heart**
and one hand on your **lower belly.**

These are your centers of **truth** and **ground.**
Hold them gently.

Let your breath flow between them—up, down, up again.
As you breathe, whisper:

"I return to balance."
"I return to balance."
"I return to balance."

---

3. Weigh the Heart

Now, ask in silence—or aloud:

"What in me is too heavy to be carried forward?"
"What truth have I swallowed that wants to rise?"
"Where am I living out of rhythm with what I know?"

Let the answers come.
Not from thought—but from sensation, image, memory, breath.

You are not looking for punishment.
You are listening for **imbalance.**
Ma'at does not accuse.
She *reveals what is out of tune*—so you can return.

Breathe. Receive. Let what is ready rise.

---

4. Name One Point of Return

Ask:

"What would bring me back into alignment right now?"

It may be something small:
Telling the truth.
Resting.
Setting a boundary.
Letting go of urgency.

Hold that one act in your awareness. Feel its weight **lighten** the body.
This is the medicine.
This is the shift.

---

5. Seal the Act

Place both hands over your heart.

Say aloud:

**"My heart is light.
My truth is clear.
My rhythm is restored."**

Bow your head.

Let a breath pass through your whole body—
as if Ma'at herself were flowing through you,
rethreading what was tangled.

Use this ritual whenever you feel:

- Scattered

- Out of sync

- Overcommitted

- Internally conflicted

- Unclear in a decision

- Pressured to perform or respond quickly

It is not the feather that brings balance.
It is **your willingness to return to it.**

Embodiment Key

The Law of Sacred Order (Ma'at)

Mantra

"I return to balance."

Simple. Direct. Sacred.

This mantra is not a declaration of perfection—
it is a vow to come back.
To pause the spiral.
To break the pattern.
To choose again.

Say it aloud when:

- You feel overwhelmed, rushed, or emotionally scattered

- You're tempted to react, perform, or please

- You've overridden your body's signal or your heart's truth

- You are entering a space that has pulled you out of rhythm in the past

This phrase calls your energy **back into order.**
It reminds your field that **your return is the healing.**

Gesture

One hand on the heart, one hand on the lower belly

This is not just a grounding posture—it is a **ritual map.**

The **heart** holds your emotional truth.
The **belly** holds your center of instinct and stability.

When both are connected by the hands,
your awareness begins to bridge emotion and embodiment.

Use this gesture to:

- Feel if your upper truth and lower knowing are in agreement

- Breathe through moments of stress or decision

- Anchor yourself when speaking a boundary or truth

- Regulate energy before action, expression, or rest

Hold the posture.
Breathe slowly.
Let the body remember what inner alignment feels like.

Anchor Use

Use the Mantra + Gesture as a full-body recalibration.

When to use:

- In the car, before a conversation

- Sitting on the edge of the bed, first or last thing in the day

- After a difficult moment when you feel pulled in too many directions

- Anytime you feel foggy, reactive, or uncentered

Repeat the mantra softly while holding the gesture.
Three deep breaths.
That's all it takes to shift your frequency.

A Living Reminder

The more you use these tools—**with presence**—
the more powerful they become.
Like a tuning fork that grows clearer with use,
they will begin to realign you the moment you invoke them.

In time, the body won't just remember Ma'at—
it will *become* her.

3. The Principle of Living Word (Heka)

Sacred Insight

To speak is to cast a spell.

In the temples of Kemet, **Heka** was not a metaphor.
It was a force. A god. A law.
The priests and priestesses of old knew:
Speech was not noise.
It was **power.**

They spoke with purpose because they understood:
To speak is to shape reality.
To name is to give life.
To declare is to direct.

Words were not decoration.
They were **instruments of creation**—woven from vibration, breath, and will.

Heka is the magic of the **Living Word.**
It is not about saying the "right" thing.
It is about speaking from a place of **energetic integrity.**

Your voice is an extension of your field.
Your breath carries your frequency.
Every word you speak carries instruction to the unseen:

- It shapes the air around you.

41

- It programs your body.

- It teaches the world how to respond to you.

- It reveals what you believe—about yourself, about others, about life.

And what is repeated, becomes **reality.**

The ancient glyph for "Heka" includes the symbol for the **twisted flax rope—**
a cord that binds and weaves.
Because speech binds energy to form.
It ties idea to reality.
It **weaves thought into existence.**

You are always casting spells.
The only question is—**are you doing it consciously?**

To live by the Principle of Living Word is to treat language as sacred.
To speak with *awareness of vibration.*
To recognize that every word either **builds or breaks.**
Heals or harms.
Contracts or liberates.

There are no neutral words.

This is not about being careful.
It is about being **consecrated.**
To speak as the ancient ones spoke—
with clarity, with will, and with *reverence for resonance.*

Words are breath made visible.
And **breath is spirit.**

So when you speak—
you are invoking the unseen.

Practical Teaching

How Language Shapes Consciousness and Reality

Your words are not commentary. They are commands.

Most people believe they are describing reality when they speak.
They say,

"I'm tired."
"I'm always like this."
"This never works for me."
"I can't trust anyone."
"I'm not creative."
And they think they are stating facts.

But the initiated know:
These are not **descriptions**.
They are **decrees.**

Language is not passive. It is **programming.**
Every word you speak is a thread in the fabric of your reality.
It does not only reflect your consciousness—it **shapes** it.

When you speak, you are:

- Instructing your body how to feel

- Instructing your mind what to filter for

- Instructing your field how to vibrate

- Instructing the Unseen what to echo back to you

Your words tell your nervous system whether to open or brace.
Your words tell your subconscious what is "true" for you.

Your words teach the people around you how to treat you.
Your words magnetize experiences that match their frequency.

This is not magic.
It is mechanics.

"I can't handle this" becomes exhaustion.
"I'm always supported" becomes alignment.
"I don't know what to do" becomes confusion.
"Clarity is coming" opens the door for it to arrive.

This is the current of Heka:
Not just *what* you say, but the **energetic origin** of how you say it.

Language that arises from fear creates constriction.
Language that arises from presence creates power.
Language that arises from alignment creates clarity.

The initiate of Heka does not speak casually.
Not because she is afraid of saying the wrong thing—
but because she understands the **creative potential of her voice.**

She knows her words are not decoration.
They are **activation.**

Sacred Silence as Powerful Restraint

Just because you can speak, doesn't mean you should.

In a world addicted to noise, silence is power.

Most speak to fill space.
To soothe discomfort.
To prove knowing.
To gain control.

But the initiate of Heka learns:
Speech without alignment weakens you.
Speech with restraint strengthens you.

Because what you do not say **echoes just as powerfully** as what you do.

Silence is not absence.
It is *containment.*
It holds energy. It builds pressure.
It allows the sacred to gather **before being released.**

Think of a bow drawn before the arrow flies.
Think of the breath before the name is spoken.
That is sacred silence:
The stillness that charges the word with force.

The one who speaks from silence speaks **with weight.**
Not because she is louder—
but because her words come from **presence, not performance.**

The ancients practiced this.
They spoke less, but with greater consequence.

46

They understood that silence is where **vibration is purified.**
Where you check:

- Does this word serve truth?

- Does it carry healing or distortion?

- Am I speaking to align—or to control?

If the answer is unclear,
remain in silence.
Because silence can protect the sacred
until the word is **ready to be born.**

This is not suppression.
This is **restraint as reverence.**
It is the knowing that every word is a release of energy—
and that you are **responsible** for where that energy flows.

At first, silence may feel unfamiliar.
It may even feel frightening.

We are conditioned to fill space.
To prove we are engaged.
To soothe discomfort with words.

To sit in sacred silence requires a **repatterning of the nervous system—**
a willingness to face the stillness we usually outrun.

You may feel awkward.
You may feel impatient.
You may feel the itch to speak without reason.

This is not failure.
It is simply the residue of living in a noisy world.

Stay with it.

Breathe into the silence.

Feel its weight shift from awkwardness to *presence*.

Let it reveal how often you were about to give away your power for the comfort of filling the air.

In time, silence will become **not absence, but authority.**

Not tension, but *tuning.*

Practice:

Spend one full hour—or one full interaction—where you speak only when the words rise from clarity.

Notice how much noise is reaction.

Notice how silence makes space for truth.

Crafting Intentional Speech and Soul Mantras

To speak with power, you must speak with purpose.

Your words shape your world—
but not all words carry the same weight.

Words spoken from habit carry history.
Words spoken from presence carry **power.**

To speak with Heka is not about perfect phrasing.
It is about **energetic integrity.**
It is about speaking from alignment—
from the core of what is true, not the surface of what is urgent.

What is Intentional Speech?

Intentional speech is **language in rhythm with your soul.**
It is speech that is:

- Rooted in clarity

- Aligned with your values

- Energetically clean—free of manipulation or self-abandonment

- Spoken with awareness of its *effect* on both self and other

You speak not to control, but to **create.**
You speak not to fill space, but to **shape it.**
You speak as one who knows:
Your word is your wand.

Presence in Light Speech: Holding Power Even in the Small

Living by the Principle of Living Word does not mean turning every conversation into a sermon.
It does not mean severing from casual joy, laughter, or simple kindness.

Small talk—the easy flow of words that builds connection—is not a violation of sacred speech.
Presence is the dividing line.

When words arise lightly but with presence, they nourish relationships.
They create bridges.
They bring a thread of ease into the weaving of daily life.

But when words are used to escape the self—
when they come from anxiety, performance, or the need to fill silence—
they **leak energy.**
They **dilute the field.**

The initiate of Heka does not fear lightness.
The danger is not levity—it is disconnection.

So even in the smallest conversations, remain rooted:

- Feel the body.

- Breathe before speaking.

- Let words rise from connection, not compulsion.

In this way, even the simplest hello becomes an act of **intentional resonance.**

Key Reflection:

Am I speaking to connect—or to escape discomfort?
Am I present to what I say—or scattering energy into the noise?

What is a Soul Mantra?

A soul mantra is a short, charged phrase that carries your **core truth** and **desired frequency.**
It is not a wish.
It is a **remembrance.**
It anchors you to the vibration you choose to embody.

It might sound like:

- *"I speak only what I am willing to receive."*

- *"I walk in clarity and truth."*

- *"My voice shapes the field around me."*

- *"I only cast spells I want to live inside."*

These phrases are not affirmations.
They are **activations.**
Each time you speak them, you are aligning thought, energy, and sound.
You are issuing a frequency that calls reality into form.

Practice: Crafting Your Living Word
Write one sentence that reflects the energy you choose to embody.
Speak it aloud, slowly.
Then ask:

- *Does this feel clean?*

- *Does this feel true?*

- *Would I want this to shape my life?*

If yes—this is your mantra.
Speak it before important moments.
Write it on your mirror.
Let it become part of your field.

Words are breath made visible.
So let your speech carry only what you are willing to breathe into your future.

In the earlier gates, the word was given to you—
a truth to remember, a law to walk by.

But here, at the threshold of **Heka**, the living word must arise **from within.**

It cannot be handed to you.
It must be chosen, claimed, and breathed into life.
For no one can speak your frequency but you.
No one can name the vibration you are here to anchor.

This is why the mantra cannot be assigned.
It must be **remembered from inside your own being.**

To speak with power is to craft your frequency with intention.
You are not merely repeating sacred law.
You are **weaving it into your own breath.**

Ritual: Naming the Flame

Consecrating the Living Word through Fire and Breath

Purpose:

To activate the chosen soul mantra by speaking it into flame—
binding vibration to the seen and the unseen,
charging the field with conscious intent.

This is not mere symbolism.
This is *spellcraft in its oldest, purest form.*

You Will Need:

- A candle (white, gold, or blue—colors of spirit and breath)

- A quiet space

- Your crafted soul mantra (written or remembered)

- Matches or a lighter

1. Prepare the Space

Dim the lights.
Place the candle before you.
Hold the mantra in your hand or heart.
Sit upright, relaxed but alert.

Take three slow, steady breaths.
With each breath, imagine gathering all scattered energy back into
your center.

Let the room become a **chamber of breath and will.**

53

2. Light the Flame

Strike the match or flick the lighter slowly.
As the flame rises, whisper:

"I awaken the fire that carries the Word."

Gaze into the flame softly.
See it not as burning, but as **living.**
It is the mirror of your breath.
It is the gate through which your Word will pass.

3. Speak the Word Into Flame

Bring the mantra into your mouth—but do not rush.
Let it gather weight.

When ready, speak your crafted mantra aloud.
Clearly. Slowly. As if placing it into the hands of the unseen.

Speak it three times:

- First time: for your body

- Second time: for your mind

- Third time: for your spirit

Let each repetition carry more presence, more certainty.

Feel the vibration moving from chest to mouth to flame.
Feel it entering the current of reality.

4. Seal the Spell

Place your right hand lightly over your heart.
Bow your head slightly.

Whisper:

"Let it be spoken.
Let it be woven.
Let it be done."

Blow out the flame with reverence.
Not as an ending—
but as a sending.

Your Word now lives within you—
and beyond you.

Afterward:

Carry the mantra forward:

- Speak it in the morning to align the field.

- Whisper it before stepping into important spaces.

- Breathe it silently when doubt arises.

Each time you speak it, you strengthen its frequency—
not as a wish, but as a command written in breath.

Your Word is no longer theory.
It is active.
It is living.
It is law.

Embodiment Key

The Principle of Living Word (Heka)

Mantra

Your chosen Living Word.

The mantra you crafted and consecrated is now your guide.
It is not a decoration.
It is a **frequency you embody.**

Each time you speak it, you reassert your alignment.
Each time you breathe it, you adjust your field.

This mantra is not for show.
It is for sovereignty.

Gesture

Hand from Mouth to Heart

Simple, sacred, powerful:

- As you speak your Living Word, place your right hand gently over your mouth.

- Then, as you finish the phrase, move the hand slowly to rest over your heart.

This movement seals the word into your body:
from breath (mouth)
into energy (heart).

It reminds the nervous system:
"What I speak, I must carry."

Use the gesture:

- When you feel the temptation to speak carelessly

- When you are preparing to speak into manifestation

- When you are sealing a decision, an intention, or a prayer

Anchor Use

In moments of choice, speak your Living Word with the Gesture.

- Before meetings, conversations, or performances

- Before setting intentions, beginning rituals, or closing cycles

- In moments of inner conflict, confusion, or fear of speaking

Bring your awareness back to the Living Word.
Let it recalibrate your vibration before you shape your reality through voice.

**You will find that the more often you root into it, the less you need to search for the right words—
the Word will arise from you naturally.**

Living Reminder:
The Word grows stronger through use.
The more you speak from alignment,
the more the world speaks back to you in the language of truth.

Thus the Law of Heka is sealed:
You are no longer merely a speaker.
You are a shaper.

4. The Law of the Mirror

Sacred Insight

As within, so without.
As above, so below.

There is no outside.
There is no inside.
There is only reflection.

The ancient initiates understood:
The world you see is the world you are.

Not because reality is an illusion—
but because it is a **response.**

The external is the echo of the internal.
The visible is the shadow of the invisible.

Your life is not happening *to* you.
It is happening *through* you.
It is a mirror that reveals:

- The beliefs you nurture

- The energies you carry

- The agreements you have made with yourself and the
  unseen

Each person you meet, each delay, each blessing, each loss—
all are reflections of frequencies moving within you.

Some mirrors show beauty.
Some mirrors show distortion.
Both are gifts.

Both are invitations:
See clearly.
Adjust inwardly.
Shape outwardly.

The mirror does not lie—
but it does speak the language of **energy**, not identity.

You are not defined by what the mirror shows.
You are informed by it.

If you see abandonment, ask:

Where have I abandoned myself?

If you see betrayal, ask:

Where have I betrayed my own knowing?

If you see expansion, ask:

What part of me is now ready to rise?

The Law of the Mirror teaches this:
You do not heal the mirror by cleaning its surface.
You heal the mirror by shifting what it reflects.

You do not battle the reflection.
You adjust the source.

You remember:
The world is a temple of reflection.
And every reflection is an oracle.

Practical Teaching

Projection as Self-Revelation

What you react to outside reveals what you carry inside.

The world mirrors your energy.
But your projections color the glass.

Reality is not happening to you.
It is happening through you—
responding to the unseen energies you carry within.

Yet most who encounter the mirror do not see purely.
They see **through the stain of their own projections.**

Projection is what happens when unhealed emotions, suppressed truths, or forgotten powers
are **cast outward** onto others or onto life itself.

You do not see what is.
You see what you **expect**, based on what lives unexamined within.

Example:

- If you carry betrayal within, you may perceive betrayal even where none exists.

- If you fear unworthiness, you may see rejection in neutral glances.

- If you have disowned your strength, you may idolize others' power while denying your own.

The mirror is still offering a reflection—
but the reflection is **filtered** through your emotional and energetic
residues.

This is why reaction is revelation.

The stronger your reaction to something "out there,"
the more clearly it points to something stirring **in here.**

What you condemn most fiercely,
what you fear most deeply,
what you crave most desperately—
all these are **maps** to hidden parts of yourself.

The Initiate's Question:

The initiate of the Mirror does not blame the outer world.
Nor do they shame themselves for reacting.

They ask with sacred honesty:

- **What part of me is this revealing?**

- **What am I projecting onto this person, this moment, this mirror?**

- **What truth within me has been neglected, rejected, or hidden?**

This is not self-blame.
This is self-reclamation.

Every projection recognized is power reclaimed.
Every mirror read truthfully is healing begun.

You cannot cleanse the reflection by scrubbing the surface.
You cleanse it by purifying the source—the energy that shapes the seeing.

Sacred Practice:

When judgment, anger, jealousy, admiration, or fear arises—pause.

Breathe.

Do not attack the reflection.
Instead, ask:

**"What is this showing me about myself—
not to shame me, but to awaken me?"**

Listen not with defensiveness, but with curiosity.
What seems like judgment from life is often **invitation** from the soul.

In time, the world ceases to be a battlefield.
It becomes a field of revelation.
And every reflection becomes a doorway back to wholeness.

Energetic Reflection and Self-Honesty

To see clearly, you must feel clearly.

The mirror of life does not reflect your titles, your masks, or your wishes.
It reflects your **energy.**

It reveals not who you say you are—
but what you actually carry within your field.

It is not personal.
It is vibrational.

This is why self-honesty is the key.

If you refuse to feel your own energies,
you will misread the mirrors life places before you.
You will label others as the problem.
You will wage wars on reflections,
while remaining blind to the source.

Energetic reflection shows you:

- Where your fear still vibrates

- Where your belief systems distort experience

- Where your unspoken grief calls for healing

- Where your hidden potentials are waiting to be claimed

The mirror is a messenger.
It does not accuse.
It reveals.

But to read it clearly,
you must be willing to meet yourself fully.

What Self-Honesty Looks Like

- Feeling jealousy and asking:

"What unlived part of me is crying out to be expressed?"

- Feeling anger and asking:

"Where have I allowed violation of my boundaries—or betrayed them myself?"

- Feeling admiration and asking:

"What brilliance in me have I disowned or forgotten?"

Self-honesty does not mean blame.
It means taking sacred responsibility for your inner landscape—
so that you can read your outer reflection with clean sight.

The Practice of Clear Seeing:

When a mirror moment arises—
a strong emotional reaction, a repeated pattern, a sudden conflict—
pause.

Before interpreting, ask:

"What is this reflecting about my current energetic state?"
"Is this showing me a fear, a wound, a belief, or a power I have neglected?"

Let the body speak before the mind rushes in.

- Feel where tension lives.

- Feel where contraction happens.

- Feel where grief or hunger or pride stirs.

The energy will tell you more than the story.

The initiate of the Mirror becomes a seer not through judgment—
but through **intimate, radical honesty** with their own field.

Thus, the outer becomes less threatening.
Thus, reality becomes a dance, not a battle.

You are not at war with life.
You are **in dialogue with it.**

Using Triggers to Identify Misalignment

Every sharp edge you meet points to a place where you can return to wholeness.

A trigger is not a mistake.
It is a **summons**.

When something outside you stirs an outsized reaction—
rage, grief, shame, defensiveness—
you are not being cursed.
You are being **called inward**.

The mind wants to defend.
The ego wants to blame.
The story wants to justify.

But the initiate of the Mirror learns:
A trigger is not about the world's failure.
It is about your next threshold.

Each trigger is a signal:

- *Here is where your energy contracts.*

- *Here is where a wound still vibrates.*

- *Here is where your identity grips too tightly or too fearfully.*

- *Here is where healing, integration, or release can happen.*

Misalignment reveals itself through pain—
but it offers realignment through presence.

The sharper the trigger,
the more powerful the energy trapped beneath it.

The mirror is not attacking you.
It is showing you where your reflection is **fractured—**
and inviting you to restore it.

How to Work with a Trigger Sacredly

When you feel the spark of a trigger:

1. **Pause.**
   Resist the first story that rushes in.

2. **Feel.**
   Notice where in the body the trigger lives—tightness in the chest, heat in the face, knot in the gut.

3. **Inquire.**
   Ask:

"What belief is being challenged right now?"
"What part of me feels unsafe, unseen, or invalidated?"
"What story about myself or the world is this exposing?"

4. **Listen without judgment.**
   What rises may not be rational. It may be old. It may be raw.
   That is sacred material.

5. **Choose the realignment.**
   You may need to grieve, forgive, release a story, or reclaim a truth.

The trigger is not the enemy.
It is the arrow pointing back to your own lost power.

When you read triggers as maps,
the world ceases to wound you randomly—
and begins to **initiate you precisely.**

In this way, every sharp moment becomes a softening.
Every hard reflection becomes a doorway.
And every disruption becomes an opportunity to rebuild from
wholeness.

Ritual: The Three Reflections

Gazing into the Mirror to See Beyond Surface into Soul

Purpose:

To consciously engage the mirror as a sacred oracle—
to witness not just appearance,
but the energies, truths, and misalignments seeking integration.

This ritual is not about fixing the surface.
It is about seeing *through* it.

You Will Need:

- A quiet space

- A mirror (hand mirror or wall mirror)

- A journal and pen (optional but powerful)

- A soft, open breath

---

1. Prepare the Space

Dim the lights if possible.
Sit or stand comfortably before the mirror.
Let the room be silent, soft, without distraction.

Breathe slowly, steadily.
Let the breath begin to draw the mind inward.

Look at your reflection—
but do not rush to judge or label.
Simply be present to the being before you.

2. First Reflection: Surface Seeing

Gaze into your eyes.
Gently, neutrally.

Notice:

- How do I appear today?

- What emotions are visible on my surface?

- What posture, expression, tension do I carry?

Do not correct anything.
Simply *witness*.

This is the outer reflection: what the world might see at first glance.

Breathe.
Acknowledge without commentary.

3. Second Reflection: Energetic Reading

Now, soften your gaze.
Look **through** the surface.

Ask silently or aloud:

"What energy am I carrying beneath my appearance?"

Feel:

- Is there sadness tucked behind the eyes?

- Is there pride lifting the chin?

- Is there fear tightening the jaw?

- Is there softness or hardness around the heart space?

70

Do not analyze.
Feel.

Allow the reflection to reveal **not the mask, but the current beneath.**

This is the energetic mirror.

---

4. Third Reflection: Message from the Mirror

Now, close your eyes briefly.
Breathe three slow, grounding breaths.

Open your eyes again and ask:

"What message does my mirror offer me today?"

Let the answer rise without force:
a word, a sensation, an image, a knowing.

Receive it.

Even if it seems small or strange—
trust that the mirror reflects what your soul is ready to see.

This is the oracular mirror.

---

5. Seal the Seeing

When ready, place the tips of your index and middle fingers lightly on both temples.
Feel the pulse of your own seeing.

Gaze into the mirror one final time, with no judgment, only presence.

Speak aloud with clear, steady breath:

**"As within, so without.
As I see, so I shape."**

Let the words move not just through the mouth,
but through the body, through the field.

Feel them ripple outward, sealing the space between the unseen and
the seen.

The Gesture and the Word unite—
your perception becomes a creative force, not a passive reaction.

Blow a soft, deliberate breath toward the mirror—
as if offering your reflection back into wholeness.

Lower your hands.
Close your eyes.
Breathe three slow breaths to complete the rite.

You have not simply observed the world.
You have entered into conscious relationship with it.

Afterward:

You may return to the Three Reflections practice:

- When you feel triggered or fragmented

- Before important choices or conversations

- When seeking clarity about a repeating pattern

- As a weekly or monthly check-in to stay aligned

The mirror is always available.
The question is not whether it speaks—
but whether you are ready to **listen beyond the surface.**

Embodiment Key

The Law of the Mirror

Mantra

**"As within, so without.
As I see, so I shape."**

This mantra is the living seal of the Mirror.
It reminds you that you are not a passive observer of life—
you are a participant in its shaping.

When spoken with presence, it recalibrates your sight:
from judgment to revelation,
from reaction to power.

Use the mantra:

- When facing conflict or strong emotion

- When caught in self-criticism or external blame

- When seeking to understand a repeating pattern

It calls you back to sacred seeing.

Gesture

Two fingers (index and middle) gently touching both temples

This gesture frames the seat of perception.
The temples are symbolic portals—where inner knowing and outer sight converge.

When you touch both temples:

- You signal the body to balance inner and outer awareness

- You activate the space of conscious reflection

- You prepare to see clearly, not just react

Use this gesture:

- Before responding to triggering situations

- During moments of emotional reactivity

- When you need to read the energy beneath surface appearances

Hold the fingers gently, not with tension, but with reverence.

Anchor Use

Gesture + Mantra as a Sacred Pause

In moments of emotional activation:

1. Place two fingers on your temples.

2. Breathe once into the body.

3. Speak softly or inwardly:

**"As within, so without.
As I see, so I shape."**

Let the words and touch break the automatic loop of reaction.
Let them open the doorway to deeper seeing.

The more you use this sacred pause,
the more naturally your perception refines.
You will begin to read reality with precision,
and shape it with clarity.

Living Reminder:
Every reaction is an invitation.
Every reflection is a message.
What you dare to see, you are empowered to transform.

Thus the Law of the Mirror is not an idea to be understood—
but a **lens to be lived.**

5. The Veil of Isis

Sacred Insight

The final mystery is the one veiled in plain sight.

Not all truths stand naked before you.
Some are hidden not because they are lost,
but because they are **guarded.**

In the ancient temples, the goddess **Isis**—She of Ten Thousand
Names—
was not merely worshiped for her beauty, her power, or her magic.
She was revered as the **Keeper of the Veil.**

The veil is not a barrier.
It is a protection.
A sacred weaving that hides what must ripen in silence
before it can survive the gaze of the world.

The initiate is not punished by the veil.
The initiate is prepared by it.

For wisdom must be earned by readiness,
not seized by ambition.

To rip away the veil too soon is to expose the sacred to
distortion—
to profane what has not yet taken root.

Thus, Isis stands between the seeker and the deepest mysteries—
not as a gatekeeper of punishment,
but as a **guardian of timing.**

The veil protects what is sacred.
The layered truths of the soul, the cosmos, and the unseen realms cannot all be known at once.

Some truths must be approached with patience.
Some must be touched with reverence.
Some must remain wrapped in silence until the heart has widened enough to receive them.

The initiate of the Veil learns to love the not-knowing.
To dwell in mystery without forcing revelation.
To recognize that when answers are hidden, it is not because one is unworthy—
but because some knowing is too potent to be given before its hour.

In this way, Isis teaches that **patience is power.**
Reverence is readiness.
Mystery is medicine.

The veil is not against you.
It is **for you**.

And when the soul is ready,
the veil parts of its own accord.

Practical Teaching

Revelation Requires Readiness

Truth is not hidden from you. It is protected for you.

In the impatient heart, mystery feels like punishment.
The seeker demands:

"Why can I not see it now?"
"Why is the way not clear?"
"Why must I wait?"

But the Veil is not cruelty.
It is **mercy**.

The soul must grow into the truths it seeks.

A truth seen too early becomes distortion.
A wisdom grasped without preparation can shatter rather than
awaken.
A revelation forced before its time can destroy what it was meant to
heal.

Isis teaches:

"What is sacred must be unveiled, not snatched."

The initiate who tries to tear away the Veil
risks mistaking fragments for fullness,
symbols for substance,
desire for destiny.

True revelation is not something you chase.
It is something you become ready to receive.

You are not waiting on the truth.
The truth is waiting on *you*—
on your readiness to hold it without distortion, without agenda,
without fear.

The Signs of Readiness

You know you are nearing revelation when:

- The need to control softens into willingness to trust.

- The hunger for certainty quiets into patient curiosity.

- The grasping loosens, and you become *available* instead of
  aggressive.

Revelation arrives **when the vessel is spacious enough to
contain it.**
When the soul can hold the new frequency without collapsing the
old structures.

Thus, every moment of silence, every unanswered prayer, every
delayed sign
is not rejection.
It is preparation.

The Veil is not delaying you.
It is **refining you.**

Sacred Reflection:

When you find yourself asking, *"Why can I not see?"*
Ask instead:

"Where am I still hardening against mystery?"
"Where can I soften into greater trust?"

Mystery does not block the path.
Mystery *is* the path.

Feminine Mystery: Stillness, Waiting, and Attunement

Some truths do not shout. They unfold in silence.

The sacred is not seized through force.
It is revealed through **attunement**.

Just as the moon does not rush to become full,
and seeds break through the earth only when the season ripens them,
so too the mysteries unfold according to **timing**,
not according to **desire**.

The feminine current—the current of Isis—is not linear.
It does not move by conquest.
It moves by **invitation and reception.**

It demands of the initiate not striving, but **stillness.**
Not pushing, but **presence.**

Stillness is not inactivity.
Stillness is attunement:
an active listening to the rhythms of the unseen.

Waiting, in the sacred sense, is not passive.
It is preparation.

While the impatient mind judges silence as failure,
the attuned heart knows:
every breath of waiting is preparing the vessel.

You do not grow into mysteries by demanding answers.
You grow into them by tuning your entire being
to the subtle frequencies that whisper behind the veil.

How to Attune to Mystery

Attunement begins with surrendering the demand to know.
It moves into *listening for what already surrounds you.*

- Notice the patterns repeating in dreams, symbols, conversations.

- Sense the energetic shifts before they crystallize into events.

- Feel where life is pulsing "yes" and where it quietly withdraws.

- Trust that absence can speak as clearly as presence.

Mystery speaks.
But only those who listen beyond language can hear it.

Sacred Reflection:

Instead of asking, *"How do I unveil the mystery?"*
Ask:

"How can I become more available to the unveiling?"
"Where can I deepen my listening?"
"How can I honor what is not yet ready to be known?"

The initiate of the Veil learns not to tear open the hidden—
but to **become so attuned, so reverent, so trusting,**
that truth blooms naturally,
like a flower opening at the first kiss of sun.

How to Read Omens, Symbols, and Concealed Messages

The hidden speaks. You must learn how to listen.

When revelation is not yet ready to unfold in full,
it begins by sending **symbols**.

Life speaks first in riddles,
in glimpses,
in patterns too delicate for the mind but clear to the attuned soul.

Symbols rarely announce themselves loudly.
They arrive like subtle invitations—threads of meaning woven
through daily life.

You may feel the presence of a symbol through:

- A word or image that stirs an unexpected feeling

- A dream that lingers in the body longer than the mind can
  explain

- An animal, object, or pattern appearing at a moment of
  heightened energy

- A song, phrase, or image arriving exactly when the heart is
  asking

- A sudden internal knowing that refuses to be dismissed

These are only examples.
In truth, **all of life is speaking.**
Every encounter, every delay, every repetition, every stirring of the
heart—
all are pages of the hidden text,
waiting for the initiate to read.

The mind will often try to ignore these threads.
The soul recognizes them instantly.

Symbols are not proof to the mind.
They are nourishment for the spirit.

The more reverently you notice,
the more clearly the unseen begins to speak.

The unseen world does not remain silent—
but it speaks in the **language of layers**.

To walk the path of the Veil is to **become literate** in this symbolic language.

Omens, dreams, synchronicities, intuitive nudges—
these are not accidents.
They are **early echoes** of truths moving toward the surface.

They are the way the sacred tests your attentiveness:

Will you honor what whispers, or only what shouts?

How to Read the Hidden Language

Reading symbols is not about superstition.
It is about *relationship.*

You do not extract meanings like facts.
You **listen** to them, as you would to a wise elder speaking in poetry.

Ask yourself:

- What feeling rises when this symbol appears?

- What personal myth or story is this symbol activating in me?

- What pattern or theme is repeating around me right now?

- If this were a message, what part of my path would it be illuminating?

Symbols do not often explain themselves immediately.
They **open doors** inside you—
doors you must be willing to walk through with curiosity, not demand.

The more you respect the small signs,
the more life entrusts you with larger revelations.

Ignore the symbols, and the deeper truths retreat.
Honor them, and they lead you home.

Sacred Practice: Symbol Tracking

For seven days, keep a small notebook or sacred space on your phone:

- Record any signs, dreams, repeated numbers, animals, phrases, or intuitive flashes.

- Notice patterns without trying to force meaning.

- Let the language of the hidden reveal itself over time.

Symbolic literacy is not built through instant understanding—
it is built through **relationship and remembrance.**

Thus the initiate of the Veil learns:
The sacred does not always speak directly.
But it always speaks.

The question is:

Will you remain attuned long enough to hear?

Ritual: Reading the Hidden Text

Divining the Message Concealed Beneath the Seen

Purpose:

To practice receiving guidance from behind the Veil—
to ask not for certainty,
but for the symbol that speaks to the soul's next unfolding.

This ritual is not about finding answers.
It is about **entering sacred dialogue with mystery itself.**

You Will Need:

- A quiet space

- A sacred book, oracle deck, journal, or even a poetry book (anything you trust to carry living energy)

- A candle (optional, but powerful to represent inner illumination)

- Your breath and willingness to listen

---

1. Prepare the Space

Light the candle, if using.
Place the sacred text (book, oracle, journal) before you.

Sit comfortably.
Close your eyes.
Take three slow breaths—each one deeper than the last.

Whisper within:

**"I open myself to the language behind the veil.
Show me what I am ready to receive."**

---

2. Whisper Your Question

Silently—or aloud—speak a soft, simple question to the unseen.

It might be:

- *"What truth am I ready to remember?"*

- *"What energy is unfolding in me now?"*

- *"What guidance lies hidden before me?"*

Or any question that rises from the heart.
Keep it simple, pure, without demand.

You are not interrogating the sacred.
You are inviting it.

---

3. Draw or Open

If using a book:
Let your hands hover lightly over the closed pages.
When you feel a subtle pull or heat or sense of "now"—
open to a random page.

Let your eyes fall where they will.

If using cards:
Shuffle slowly, reverently.
Pull one card when you feel the breath of readiness.

If using your journal:
Turn to a past entry.
Let memory itself become your symbol.

4. Read with the Inner Eye

Do not over-analyze what you receive.
You are not looking for literal answers.

Read the words, see the images, feel the impression—
and ask:

"What layer of this speaks to my current path?"
"What energy is being mirrored back to me?"

Allow the meaning to unfold symbolically, not logically.
Sometimes the true message will bloom hours or days later.

Trust that the act of asking and receiving has already shifted your
field.

5. Seal the Exchange

When ready, lift one open hand before your face.
Hold it an inch away from the skin.
With slow, deliberate reverence, sweep your hand horizontally
across your face—
as if parting an invisible veil.

As your hand moves, whisper aloud:

"I honor the hidden.
I trust the unveiling."

Feel the space between the seen and unseen breathe open.

If you wish, after the sweep,
place your hand lightly over your heart to anchor the feeling into
your body.

Blow out the candle, if lit.
Close the sacred text slowly, with both hands.

You have not forced revelation.
You have become available to it.

In this way, you do not rip answers from the unseen.
You walk beside mystery, hand in hand,
with the patience of the ancient ones.

Embodiment Key

The Veil of Isis

Mantra

**"I honor the hidden.
I trust the unveiling."**

This mantra reminds you:
You are not abandoned by truth.
You are being refined by mystery.

Each time you speak it, you affirm your readiness:

- To listen without forcing

- To walk without grasping

- To wait with sacred attentiveness

The mantra softens the restless mind and aligns the heart with the natural rhythms of revelation.

Gesture

The Sacred Sweep Across the Face

Slowly sweep your open hand horizontally across your face—
an inch away from the skin—
as if parting an invisible veil.

- The hand does not rush.

- The motion is slow, soft, deliberate.

This Gesture awakens the space between seen and unseen.
It reminds the body that revelation is a process of allowing, not seizing.

Use the Gesture:

- When you feel impatient for answers

- When confusion clouds the path

- When you need to return to reverence and trust

The sweep calls back the sacred rhythm of unfolding.

Anchor Use

Gesture + Mantra as an Act of Trust

When mystery feels heavy, when clarity feels far away:

1. Pause.

2. Lift your open hand.

3. Sweep it slowly across your face.

4. Whisper or inwardly breathe the mantra:

**"I honor the hidden.
I trust the unveiling."**

Let this act remind every cell in your body:

The unseen is not your enemy.
It is your initiator.

Over time, the Gesture and the Mantra weave a new pattern into your field—
the pattern of sacred patience, receptive wisdom, and deep inner trust.

Living Reminder:
Mystery is not the absence of answers.
It is the presence of energies still taking shape.

Thus the initiate of the Veil walks not by force,
but by attunement, patience, and holy trust.

6. The River of Becoming (Hapi's Law)

Sacred Insight

Stagnation is illusion—only flow is truth.

There is no stillness in the living world.
Only flow concealed beneath appearances.

Even the stone is shifting.
Even the seed in the dark is becoming.
Even your breath, unnoticed, is reshaping you with every exhale.

Hapi, the Nile, was more than a river to the ancient ones.
He was a god.
A current.
A sacred pulse that brought fertility, destruction, rebirth, and nourishment all at once.

To align with Hapi is to align with **truth in motion**.

Stagnation is a lie the mind tells when it resists movement.
But nothing sacred stands still.
The soul is shaped not by what stays,
but by what flows.

Even loss is flow.
Even grief is movement.
Even stillness has an undercurrent,
pulling you toward your becoming.

94

Those who resist the river suffer.
Not because the river is cruel,
but because they are clinging to stones
that were never meant to be held.

Change is not chaos.
It is sacred choreography.

You are not meant to harden.
You are meant to be reshaped—
again and again—until the form of your soul matches its original
design.

The initiate of the River learns to trust the current,
even when the direction is unclear.

They no longer worship certainty.
They bow to becoming.

Practical Teaching

Flow as Surrender and Power Simultaneously
To surrender is not to lose power, but to enter it fully.

In the modern world, power is often mistaken for force.
For domination.
For control.

But in the ancient ways, **power is movement in harmony** with
what already flows.
Not the building of dams, but the shaping of channels.

Hapi, god of the Nile, was not tamed—
but he was honored.
Not grasped, but **partnered with**.

The priests of the river did not demand when the waters would rise.
They attuned.
They waited.
They prepared the land to receive.

Because they knew:
You do not fight the river.
You build your life upon its rhythm.

Surrender is not weakness.
It is wisdom.

It is the knowing that life is larger than the ego's timing—
and that the current will carry you farther than your own pushing
ever could.

96

To surrender to the river is to trust:

- That becoming takes time

- That direction may shift

- That your task is not to dictate the flow,
  but to listen for where it wants to take you next

The Strength Within Surrender

It takes strength to stop resisting.
To stop grasping for control, and instead ask:

"Where is the current already moving?"
"What part of me is trying to hold the shore instead of letting go?"

Power does not always feel like fire.
Sometimes it feels like **water through stone**—
slow, steady, unstoppable.

To live by Hapi's law is to no longer demand "answers" before moving.
It is to step into motion **while becoming**.

You flow *because* it is right—
not because it is safe.
Not because it is certain.

Thus, the initiate learns:
Surrender is sacred alignment.
And movement is a form of devotion.

Emotional Release as Sacred Offering

The river does not judge what it carries. It only moves.

Your emotions are not errors.
They are expressions of movement,
signals from the soul that something is rising, ready to shift, to be
seen, to be released.

Most are taught to fear this rising.
To harden when the waters swell—
to suppress tears, swallow anger, disguise grief, deny joy.

But emotion is not weakness.
Emotion is **energy in motion.**

When you deny that motion, it becomes stagnation.
When you honor it, it becomes **flow.**

To feel is not to fall.
To feel is to move.

And to move is to trust that your becoming is already underway.

The initiate of the river learns to let emotion come,
not as a storm to be controlled,
but as a **sacred offering—**
a way of participating in the ever-unfolding current of life.

A Practice of Sacred Emotional Offering

When a strong emotion rises—especially if it feels overwhelming,
raw, or "too much"—

you are being invited into movement.
Not to perform. Not to solve.
But to **offer**.

This is not a coping mechanism.
This is **ritual presence.**

---

1. Create the Container

Step away, if you can.
Let this be a sacred pause, not a reactive outburst.
You may stand, sit, or kneel. Eyes open or closed.
You are entering a **chamber of feeling**.

---

2. Breathe and Locate

Bring your hand to your heart or your lower belly.
Breathe slowly, not to calm but to connect.

Notice where the emotion lives:

- A tightening in the throat

- A flutter in the gut

- A heat behind the eyes

You are not rushing to "fix" it.
You are **honoring its presence**.

---

3. Drop Beneath the Story

The mind will try to explain or justify. Let it rest.
Ask instead:

"What part of me is rising now?"
"What is this energy asking to release?"

Let the emotion be **sensation**, not narrative.
Allow it to move **as breath, as heat, as water.**

---

4. Offer It

When the emotion crests—when you have felt enough to name or witness it—
speak inwardly or aloud:

"I give this to the river."

Visualize Hapi's current before you.
See the emotion—color, weight, movement—leaving your field.
Entering the water.
Becoming part of flow.

Not rejected.
Not solved.
Released.

---

5. Close the Offering

Place your palms together or rest them on your lap.
Breathe in silence.
Let the quiet after the storm be your new ground.

You may feel lighter, emptier, or simply more honest.

Whatever remains is exactly enough.

This is not escape.
This is sacred circulation.

Emotion becomes prayer.
Release becomes devotion.

You have not lost control.
You have reclaimed movement.

How Resistance Blocks Prosperity

The river is not withholding. You are gripping the shore.

Prosperity is not a reward.
It is a natural result of **alignment with flow.**

Just as the Nile delivers its nourishment where the land is open,
so too does life deliver its blessings where the soul is **receptive.**

But when you resist change—
when you grip, control, postpone, or harden—
you create dams in your field.
You interrupt the current that would have carried you forward.

This resistance may appear as:

- Clinging to old identities

- Refusing to feel what wants to move

- Waiting for guarantees before acting

- Overthinking instead of trusting the next pull

And then you say: *"Why is nothing flowing?"*

But the flow is not gone.
It is simply **blocked by your own fear.**

The river is not punishing you.
It is waiting for your release.

Prosperity is Movement

Prosperity—whether in love, health, wealth, or vision—
is not something you hunt or demand.
It is something that **arrives** when you are in rhythm with your
becoming.

If you are gripping the banks,
if you are clinging to a version of yourself that no longer fits,
there is no space for the new to land.

"Why isn't the next step coming?"
"Why isn't the opportunity appearing?"

Ask instead:

"Where am I refusing to move?"
"What am I still trying to control?"
**"What am I afraid to let go of, even though it's already leaving
me?"**

You do not need to know where the river leads.
You need only to stop **clinging to where it left you.**

When you release,
even before you're ready,
you create space for life to flow again.

You send a signal to the unseen:

**"I trust the current.
I trust the becoming."**

And the river responds.

Ritual: The Offering of Flow

Releasing into Water What You No Longer Need to Hold

Purpose:

To surrender what is heavy, stagnant, or unspoken
into the element of flow—
awakening movement, trust, and the prosperity that follows release.

This is not symbolic only.
Water is a living current.
What you give it, it carries.

You Will Need:

- A small bowl of water **(or access to moving water: stream, sink, ocean, bath)**

- Quiet space

- Your breath

- A moment of truth you are ready to name and let go

---

1. Prepare the Water

Place the bowl before you.
If using natural water (river, ocean, bath), approach it with presence.

Breathe slowly.
Feel the weight of what you've been carrying.

This may be:

- An emotion

- A decision you're avoiding

- A belief that no longer fits

- A version of yourself you've outgrown

You do not need to explain it.
Only **name it inwardly**.

Let it rise.

---

2. Whisper Into the Water

When ready, bend gently toward the water.
Bring your mouth close.

Whisper, softly and with presence:

**"This no longer belongs to me.
I give it to the river."**

Speak your offering into the water—
not loudly, not with drama,
but with full sincerity.

Let the breath carry the weight out of your body
and into the waiting current.

---

3. Release the Water

If using a bowl:
Stand, walk, and pour the water into earth, sink, or stream.
Pour slowly.
Let the motion be a declaration.

If already at moving water:
Dip your hands in and let the current take it.
Or tip the vessel into the flow.

As the water leaves, whisper:

"Let it be carried.
Let it become something new."

You do not follow it.
You let it go.

---

4. Return to Stillness

After releasing the water, return to your seat.

Place one hand just above your heart.
With presence, **trace a slow, flowing wave across your chest—**
from left to right.
This is the gesture of river-memory—of choosing movement over
fear.

As your hand moves, speak aloud:

"I am the river.
I trust my becoming."

Let the words vibrate through your body like a new current
awakening within you.
Let them recalibrate your field to trust, not grasping.

Breathe.

You have not just released emotion.
You have **returned to your sacred motion.**

This is not an act of abandonment.
It is an act of trust.

What you have released is not lost.
It is returned to the current of becoming.

And now,
you are ready for what comes next.

Embodiment Key

The River of Becoming (Hapi's Law)

Mantra

"I am the river.
I trust my becoming."

This mantra is not a reminder.
It is a reorientation.
It calls you out of resistance and back into rhythm.

Use this mantra:

- When facing uncertainty or delay

- When caught in fear, control, or emotional overwhelm

- When stepping into transition, grief, or rebirth

Speak it aloud or inwardly to soften the need to grasp
and return to the sacred truth:
You are already moving.

Gesture

Flowing Hand Across the Chest

With one open hand, trace a slow, wave-like motion across your chest,
from left to right—just above the heart.

Let it be fluid, soft, sacred.
Let the motion be **felt**, not just performed.

This gesture reminds the body that **movement is safety**,
that flow is the natural state of life and soul.

Use this gesture:

- When tempted to freeze, force, or grasp

- When emotions rise and clarity recedes

- When affirming trust in the next step—before knowing what it is

---

Anchor Use

Gesture + Mantra as a Reset into Flow

In moments of tension, contraction, or confusion:

1. Pause.

2. Trace the gesture slowly across your chest.

3. Speak or breathe:

**"I am the river.
I trust my becoming."**

Let it not just calm you—
but **return you**
to the current that never stopped moving beneath your resistance.

Living Reminder:
Flow is not found.
Flow is remembered.

You do not need to chase clarity.
You need only to stop gripping the shore.

Thus the initiate of Hapi walks not in certainty,
but in sacred motion.
And everything they touch becomes part of the current.

7. The Path of the Phoenix

Sacred Insight

You are both ash and flame.

There comes a moment on every sacred path
when the life you have built
becomes too small for the soul you are becoming.

The walls crack.
The forms wither.
The names you wore so proudly begin to fall away like smoke in
wind.

This is not failure.
This is fire.

The Phoenix does not die because it is weak.
It burns because it is faithful to its own unfolding.

Long before it became the legend of later ages,
this mystery was known in Kemet—
where the sacred bird was called **Bennu**:
the soul of Ra, the pulse of rebirth,
the one who rises from the waters and the ash.

The Bennu does not fear the flame.
It enters it willingly, knowing that only through fire
can the next life be born.

Rebirth is not a reward.
It is a **consequence of courage—**
the courage to allow everything false, outdated, and heavy
to be consumed by sacred flame.

You are not here to maintain what was.
You are here to be **reborn through what must end.**

The fire reveals:

- The masks you no longer need

- The fears you no longer serve

- The cages you once mistook for homes

It takes from you only what was never truly yours.

You are not just the one who burns.
You are the one who rises.

But rise you cannot,
until you allow the old feathers to become ash.

The initiate of the Phoenix does not worship endings.
They **honor them**.
They tend the sacred fire with reverence,
trusting that nothing essential can be taken—
only purified.

They know:

That which can burn away, must.
That which remains, becomes the wings.

Thus the true rebirth does not come from clinging to what was. It comes from surrendering to the fire of what is **becoming.**

Practical Teaching

False Identities as Spiritual Burdens
The fire comes to free you, not to harm you.

You are not born with names, roles, and masks.
You are given them.
You accept them.
You build your life around them.

But as the soul expands,
what once protected you becomes a cage.

False identities are the heaviest burdens you carry.
Not because they are evil—
but because they are too small for who you are becoming.

They include:

- Roles adopted to earn love or approval

- Masks worn to survive environments of misunderstanding

- Stories of limitation accepted as destiny

- Personas clung to out of fear of the unknown

At first, these identities feel like safety.
Later, they feel like suffocation.

The fire does not come to punish you.
It comes to liberate you.

It comes to burn away what is too heavy, too tight, too false—
so that what is essential can rise, unbound.

How to Recognize a False Identity

Ask yourself:

"What part of me am I afraid to outgrow?"
"What label or role feels exhausting to maintain?"
"Where am I clinging to who I was, instead of trusting who I am becoming?"

The answers will not always be comfortable.
They are not meant to be.

Comfort is not the goal of the Phoenix.
Truth is.

You may grieve these false selves.
You may mourn the roles you must lay down.

This is sacred.
It means the fire has touched you.
It means the wings are remembering themselves beneath the ash.

Sacred Practice: Releasing the Names

As you move through this path, begin to whisper within yourself:

"I am willing to release what is no longer true."

Not because you hate what was—
but because you love what you are becoming more.

Thus the initiate of the Phoenix steps into the fire,
not to be destroyed,
but to be unbound.

Sacred Destruction as Part of the Divine Cycle

The fire clears what must fall, so the true can rise.

In the sacred architecture of the cosmos,
destruction is not the opposite of creation.
It is part of it.

There is no becoming without unraveling.
There is no rising without some surrender to ash.

The ancient ones knew:

- The Nile floods before it feeds.

- The sun must set before it rises again.

- The body must die for the soul to remember itself fully.

Thus, when the fire arrives, it is not an interruption of life.
It is life in one of its most sacred forms.

**Endings are not evidence that something has gone wrong.
They are the evidence that something new seeks to be born.**

But to the uninitiated mind, destruction feels like betrayal.
It feels like failure, loss, rejection.

The initiate must learn to see differently:

- That what burns was already decaying.

- That what falls away was no longer fit to carry the next
  unfolding.

- That what feels like death is often a **rite of realignment**.

117

The Alchemy of Sacred Ending

Ask yourself:

"What in my life is being undone, not to harm me, but to reveal me?"
"What losses or collapses have actually freed a truer part of me?"

Often, the greatest griefs are gateways.
Often, the darkest hours are doorways.

The Phoenix does not mourn the ash.
It **uses it.**

Ash becomes soil.
Ash becomes nourishment.
Ash becomes memory, wisdom, ground.

Thus the initiate learns:

Destruction is not the end of the story.
It is the clearing of the field for a truer harvest.

You are not what falls away.
You are what **remains, rises, and remembers**.

Rising from Loss, Endings, and Ego Deaths

The one who rises is not the one who burned.

After the fire, there is a silence.
A breathless space where the old names have fallen away,
but the new form is not yet clear.

This is the sacred in-between.
It is here that most seek to rebuild too quickly—
to grasp for old masks,
to rush to define the self again.

But the Phoenix rises **not by rebuilding** what was lost.
It rises by **allowing what is true to emerge unforced**.

You are not rising to become who you were.
You are rising to become who you have always been.

Endings do not empty you.
They unveil you.

And yet, many initiates ask:

"How do I know if I am in the fire?"
"How do I trust that this pain is a passage—not a punishment?"

Sacred Signs of the Phoenix Fire

The fire may come disguised as:

- The loss of a relationship you once thought would define
  you

- The collapse of a career or role you had wrapped your
  worth around

119

- The disillusionment with a path you once believed was your destiny

- The sudden clarity that an identity, community, or dream no longer fits the soul you are becoming

These are not failures.
These are sacred clearings.

The fire arrives not to destroy you—
but to **unbind you** from what cannot carry your next becoming.

In this tender phase:

- You do not need a perfect vision of what comes next.

- You do not need to "fix" the loss or explain the death.

You need only to tend the embers of your truest self.

How to Walk the Rise After Ash

Ask yourself:

"What feels alive in me now, even after the burning?"
"What am I curious to become, without needing to force it?"
"What parts of me feel weightless, free, unbound?"

Follow what feels light.
Follow what feels inevitable, not what feels urgent.

The soul does not need to be pushed into its next shape.
It unfolds—like flame reclaiming the air.

Rising is not an act of conquest.
It is an act of remembrance.

You are not inventing the next self.
You are remembering the one the fire revealed.

You are not less because you burned.
You are more.
You are essential.
You are elemental.

You are ash, yes.
But you are also flame.

Ritual: The Ash Breath

Burning the false. Breathing the new.

Purpose:

To release an outdated identity, pattern, or false self through breath and fire—
clearing the inner field for rebirth.

This ritual does not destroy you.
It releases what was never truly you to begin with.

You Will Need:

- A small piece of paper

- A pen

- A fireproof bowl or safe place to burn (candle, cauldron, or flame)

- A few quiet, undisturbed minutes

- Your breath, your truth, and your willingness

---

1. Enter the Fire Chamber

Prepare your space. Light your flame.

Sit in stillness.
Let the breath deepen.
Feel the weight of what is ready to fall away.

Not everything that has defined you is meant to come with you.

---

2. Name What No Longer Lives

Take the paper.
At the top, write:

"I release the self I no longer need."

Below that, write one identity, role, mask, or label
that you know is ready to be shed.

It may be:

- A name you've clung to out of fear

- A version of yourself shaped by survival

- A belief that you must shrink to stay safe

- A way of being that no longer fits the soul you've become

You do not need to explain it.
You only need to name it.

---

3. The Ash Breath

Hold the paper gently in your hands.

Close your eyes.

Inhale slowly.

As you exhale, whisper with your whole breath:

"From ash, I rise."

Let this be more than words.
Let it be the **breath that begins your release**.

You may repeat it three times.
Each time, deeper.
Each time, freer.

4. Burn and Offer

When you feel ready—
place the paper into the flame.

Watch it burn.

Not in drama.
In dignity.
In reverence.

As it becomes ash, say silently or aloud:

"What no longer lives in me is released."

5. Gesture and Mantra

With both hands at your lap, palms down—
raise them slowly toward your chest like wings unfolding.

As they rise, speak aloud:

"From ash, I rise."

This is the first flight.
The consecration of your next self.

You are not rushing upward.
You are *remembering* that the flame did not consume you.
It revealed you.

6. Close with Stillness

Sit.
Feel what remains.

You are not who you were.
You are not yet who you will be.

You are becoming.

And this time,
you are rising from truth.

Embodiment Key

The Path of the Phoenix

Mantra

"From ash, I rise."

This mantra is a vow to your becoming.
It is a breath that declares:

- I am not what I have lost.

- I am not what I have shed.

- I am what remains true after the burning.

Use this mantra:

- When endings feel overwhelming

- When old identities try to reclaim you

- When stepping into a new, unfamiliar version of yourself

Each time you speak it, you recalibrate your field:
from loss, to liberation.

Gesture

The Unfolding Wings

Sitting or standing,
place your hands on your lap, palms facing down.

Then slowly, with sacred breath,
raise your hands from your lap to your chest—
tracing the path of wings unfurling.

This is the rise.
This is the memory of your elemental self, returning to form.

Use this gesture:

- When mourning what has ended

- When feeling raw, lost, or undefined

- When reclaiming your own becoming, even before clarity arrives

---

Anchor Use

Gesture + Mantra as Flight from the Ashes

In moments of grief, disorientation, or new beginning:

1. Sit or stand in stillness.

2. Place your palms down on your lap.

3. Breathe in.

4. As you exhale, slowly raise your hands to your heart center, like wings unfolding.

5. Speak, aloud or inwardly:

"From ash, I rise."

Feel the breath as flame,
the hands as wings,
the soul as fire made visible.

You are not the ash.
You are the life that rises from it.

Living Reminder:
What the fire takes, it takes to reveal your truest form.
What remains after the burning was never meant to leave you.

Thus the initiate of the Phoenix no longer fears endings.
They walk with the fire as their ally,
and the rising becomes their way of life.

8. The Law of Sacred Opposition (Set & Horus)

Sacred Insight

What opposes you refines you.

There is a place in the sacred path
where what stands against you
is not a barrier—
but a teacher.

This is the place of Sacred Opposition.

Set, the force of disruption, chaos, and disorder—
and Horus, the force of restoration, clarity, and sovereignty—
are not enemies by mistake.
They are woven into the architecture of becoming.

Without Set, there is no Horus.
Without opposition, there is no refinement of vision, strength, or
will.

What resists you does not come to destroy you.
It comes to sharpen you.

The ancients of Kemet knew:
Set was not merely the villain of the myth.

He was the **necessary adversary**—
the one who hammered Horus into true kingship,
the one who burned away false claims and demanded true sight.

Opposition is not cruelty.
It is consecration.

The river does not run smooth from source to sea.
It cuts through stone.

The soul does not rise to sovereignty through ease alone.
It rises through the sacred struggle that reveals what is real.

Opposition comes to awaken your strength.
Conflict comes to awaken your clarity.
Challenge comes to awaken your sovereignty.

Not as punishment—
but as preparation.

The initiate of Sacred Opposition knows:
You are not here to avoid resistance.
You are here to meet it, face it, and be revealed by it.

Because only in the mirror of opposition
does your true face emerge.

Practical Teaching

Chaos Reveals Strength

You do not know your strength until it is summoned.

Chaos is not the enemy of the sacred.
It is its crucible.

In the mythology of Kemet,
Set—the god of disruption, chaos, and challenge—
was not banished from the cosmic order.
He was woven into it.

Set tests the soul.
Not to humiliate it,
but to **reveal** it.

**You do not truly know your strength
until you are asked to stand within the storm.**

Without chaos:

- There is no clarity of what truly matters.

- There is no anchoring of inner truth.

- There is no refinement of will.

Without resistance, the spirit remains untested—
soft, fragile, easily shattered by the first real gust.

131

The initiate understands:
Opposition is not an insult.
It is a mirror.

It reflects:

- Where you still doubt your own vision

- Where you are still attached to outcomes instead of essence

- Where your strength is not yet fully seated within you

Each encounter with disruption, conflict, or delay
is not a punishment.
It is an invitation to **stabilize deeper** inside yourself.

Sacred Practice: Standing in the Heart of Chaos

When chaos arises—
when the ground shakes, when clarity dissolves,
when reaction threatens to seize your breath—
pause.

Do not rush to act.
Do not rush to explain.
Do not rush to defend.

Still yourself like the eye of the storm.

Place a hand over your heart or your belly.
Close your eyes, even if only for a breath.

Feel your own center.
Remember that it is older than this storm.
Older than this moment.

Inwardly ask:

"What part of me is being tempered in this fire?"
"What clarity is seeking to be forged in me?"

Let the questions open space inside you.
Let them anchor you deeper than reaction.

Move not from fear.
Move not from urgency.
Move from the stability that chaos was sent to awaken in you.

Chaos is not the end of order.
It is the instrument that reveals a higher one.

Set is not the destroyer of the sacred.
He is its necessary challenger.

The soul that is refined by chaos
is the soul that rises clear, steady, and crowned.

Opposition as Refinement, Not Punishment

What stands against you reveals your hidden gold.

When opposition rises—
when you are resisted, denied, misunderstood, delayed—
the untrained soul sees punishment.
The initiate sees purification.

Opposition is not cruelty.
It is sacred compression.

It presses upon the soul's field,
testing the strength of its coherence,
forcing what is weak or fragmented to either integrate or fall away.

In the unseen world, your energy is not shaped by ease.
It is shaped by pressure.

When you meet opposition with anchored presence:

- Your field condenses and strengthens.

- Your will becomes clarified and pure.

- Your sovereign energy becomes undeniable.

When you react with fear, collapse, or resentment:

- Your field fractures.

- Energy leaks through old wounds.

- You become vulnerable to forces outside your own sacred design.

The initiate remembers:

You are still shaping reality.
You are still casting the Living Word.
You are still reading the Mirror.
You are still walking within the Law of Sacred Order.

The principles do not vanish in chaos.
They are revealed more clearly.

Opposition is not a break from the laws of becoming—
it is their sacred test.

The Hidden Alchemy of Opposition

Every sacred trial exerts force upon your energetic structure.
It demands a choice:

- To fracture and dissipate your field through reaction

- Or to stabilize and deepen your field through presence

In that moment of conscious choice,
you refine your sovereignty.

Not by overpowering the external world—
but by mastering your own internal throne.

This is the ancient path of Horus:
to rise not because Set is defeated,
but because Self is enthroned.

Opposition is not sent to destroy you.
It is sent to crown you.

The very force that seems to resist you
is the forge that reveals your true weight, your true light, your true
name.

Thus, the initiate welcomes resistance
not as a curse to escape,
but as a consecration to complete.

Duality Must Be Harmonized, Not Avoided

You do not create by fleeing tension—you create by walking through it.

The sacred path is not an escape from duality.
It is the mastery of it.

You are not here to erase conflict, resistance, or tension.
You are here to **work with them**—
to shape reality through the forces that challenge you.

You are indeed always shaping reality.
Through perception, through word, through field.
This is the truth of Dual Vision, Living Word, and Sacred Order.

But shaping reality does not mean eliminating friction.
It means shaping through the necessary forces of evolution.

Creation unfolds through tension.

This is not punishment.
It is the hidden law by which all true becoming occurs.

In the hidden architecture of existence:

- Every seed must push against the soil to emerge.

- Every river must carve through resistance to shape the land.

- Every soul must refine through trial to embody its true frequency.

Without resistance, without compression,
there would be no shaping at all—
only stagnation, diffusion, weakness.

Opposition is not failure.
Opposition is part of the creative field itself.

Thus, when you move energy—
when you reshape your field, when you call a new reality into form—
you will encounter resistance.

Not because you are wrong.
But because you are alive, in motion, and expanding.

The river meets stone because it moves.
The soul meets friction because it is growing.

If there is no resistance, there is no true creation.

If there is no opposition, there is no true rising.

Opposition does not mean you are losing.
It means you are birthing.

The friction you feel is the sacred forge refining the next true form.

Harmonizing the Sacred Forces

In the ancient myths, Set and Horus are not simply enemies.
They are the two poles of sacred evolution.

- Set awakens strength through trial.

- Horus restores vision through sovereignty.

The initiate does not choose one and exile the other.
The initiate learns to **crown both within.**

When you harmonize duality within:

- You meet resistance without collapse.

- You hold your field even when the winds rise.

- You move forward through tension without abandoning your core.

The initiate who can stand at the crossroads of chaos and clarity
without flinching, without fragmenting,
becomes the one who shapes reality from the seat of true
sovereignty.

They do not fear the opposition—
they **rise because of it.**

Ritual: Facing the Shadow

Standing steady in the fire of refinement.

Purpose:

To consciously encounter inner or outer opposition,
to meet it without collapse,
and to anchor sovereignty through breath, mantra, and gesture.

This ritual does not destroy the shadow.
It integrates the strength it was meant to awaken.

You Will Need:

- A quiet space with no interruptions

- A seated or standing posture that feels strong and alert

- A willingness to breathe through discomfort, not avoid it

- Your own presence, as your altar

---

1. Prepare the Inner Chamber

Sit or stand upright.
Feel your feet or seat rooted into the earth.
Place your hands gently on your thighs or at your sides.

Close your eyes.

Breathe deeply.
Breathe slowly.

---

2. Call the Opposition Forward

Inwardly, allow a situation, a memory, or a feeling of opposition to arise:

- A moment you were resisted, rejected, challenged.

- A fear of failure, collapse, or being misunderstood.

- A part of you that trembles before the unknown.

Do not analyze it.
Do not fight it.

Simply allow it to rise like smoke from the embers.

---

3. Stand in the Eye of the Storm

As the discomfort surfaces, do not run.
Do not collapse.

Instead:
Breathe.

Place a hand lightly over your heart.
Anchor into your center.

Feel that beneath the rising chaos,
there is something that does not move.

There is something older, steadier, deeper than fear.

Hold it.

---

4. Mantra and Gesture: The Opening of the Fists

Now, with both hands,
clench your fists tightly—as if holding all the tension, all the fear,
all the resistance.

Feel it.
Hold it consciously, not reactively.

Then, on an exhale,
slowly open your fists, spreading your fingers wide.

As you do, speak aloud or inwardly:

"What resists me refines me."

Let the breath carry away what is ready to fall.
Let the gesture seal your choice to transform, not fracture.

---

5. Sit in Sovereignty

Remain for a few breaths in silence.

Feel the steadiness growing within you—
not because the opposition vanished,
but because you are no longer at war with it.

You have become the stillness that commands the storm.

You have crowned yourself in the eye of sacred tension.

You do not defeat opposition by force.
You transmute it by presence.

You do not escape the shadow.
You integrate its strength.

This is the sovereignty of Horus born through the trial of Set.

Embodiment Key

The Law of Sacred Opposition

Mantra

"What resists me refines me."

This mantra is not a defense against difficulty.
It is a remembrance that every resistance carries the seed of refinement.

Use this mantra:

- When you feel blocked, challenged, or rejected

- When chaos rises inside or around you

- When you are tempted to collapse, attack, or flee

Each time you speak it,
you reframe the energy of opposition into fuel for your becoming.

Gesture

The Opening of the Fists

Clench your fists tightly, drawing in the tension.
Then, on a sacred breath out,
slowly open your fists, spreading your fingers wide.

This is the sacred act of conscious release:

- Not giving up

- Not fighting blindly

- But **transmuting tension into sovereignty**

Use this gesture:

- When you need to transmute stress, fear, or resistance

- When facing confrontation, challenge, or internal doubt

- When preparing to move forward through uncertainty

Anchor Use

Gesture + Mantra as Field Stabilization

When opposition rises:

1. Pause.

2. Breathe.

3. Clench your fists to gather the tension consciously.

4. Exhale and slowly open your hands wide.

5. Speak inwardly or aloud:

"What resists me refines me."

Feel the tension transmute.
Feel the field condense around your center.
Feel yourself becoming more whole—not despite resistance, but because of it.

Living Reminder:
Opposition is not a sign of failure.
It is the sacred confirmation that you are moving, shaping, and becoming.

Thus, the initiate of Sacred Opposition no longer fears the storm.
They know:
It is sharpening their wings.
It is refining their crown.
It is preparing them to walk as sovereign light in a shifting world.

9. The Crowned Self (Horus Principle)

Sacred Insight

To walk the path is to wear the crown within.

There comes a moment on the path
when you stop reaching outward.
You stop asking, "What is the rule?"
You begin asking, "What is true in me now?"

Not in rebellion.
But in remembrance.

Because you have become the very law you once sought to obey.

Horus is not the seeker.
Horus is the one who has returned.

Not from comfort,
but from initiation.
Not by avoiding shadow,
but by integrating it.

He is the sovereign soul—
not because he was born perfect,
but because he chose to rise,
again and again,
until nothing ruled him but truth.

The crown he wears is not just a symbol.
It is an energetic state:

- Clear vision.

- Aligned speech.

- Centered will.

- Sacred neutrality.

- Deep self-authority.

The initiate becomes crowned
not by being flawless—
but by becoming *whole*.

The true initiate does not follow the law.
They become it.

They have walked the fires of destruction.
They have stood in the mirror.
They have learned to see, speak, feel, and align with what is real.

Now, there is no need to search for a higher authority.
They walk as one.

To be crowned is not to dominate.
It is to embody.

To walk in the world as a living law.
Not of control—
but of coherence, clarity, and consecrated presence.

The Crowned Self does not ask for permission.
It does not wait to be chosen.
It does not shrink when misunderstood.

It walks.
It sees.
It speaks.
It shapes.

And where it goes, alignment follows.

Thus the journey ends where it truly begins:
with a being who no longer seeks sovereignty—
but who walks as the law itself.

Practical Teaching

Embodiment as the Final Step

You are not here to follow the law. You are here to walk as it.

To understand is not enough.
To feel deeply is not enough.
To believe is not enough.

The path becomes real only when it is **embodied**.

Not once. Not only in ritual.
But in the **daily act of alignment**—
in how you think, speak, choose, and carry your presence.

You are crowned not by knowledge,
but by the constancy of your coherence.

The laws you have learned—
sight, balance, speech, symbolic literacy, surrender, refinement—
are not ornaments for the mind.

They are instruments of becoming.

And to embody them means:

- You see with Dual Vision when faced with illusion.

- You restore Sacred Order when chaos tries to scatter you.

- You speak Living Word even when no one is listening.

- You interpret the Mirror before casting judgment.

- You honor the Veil of Isis when no answer arrives.

- You offer your emotion to the River instead of drowning in it.

- You let go with the Phoenix.

- You face the fire of Set without collapsing.

- And you rise, not to be worshipped—
  but to **walk as a source of alignment** wherever you are.

This is embodiment.
Not perfection.
But presence.

Not theory.
But lived resonance.

The initiate becomes crowned the moment their **inner alignment** is no longer dependent on outer conditions.

When their breath steadies the room.
When their field calms the storm.
When their yes and their no both carry clarity.
When their silence speaks.
When their word creates.

To embody is to cease striving.
It is to become magnetic to what matches your coherence—
and invisible to what does not.

You are no longer chasing truth.
You are **living it in form**.

Thus, embodiment is not the final chapter of learning.
It is the beginning of true influence.

Not through force.
But through **field**.

The world does not change when you believe.
It changes when you **embody**.

The Crown as Authority, Clarity, and Divine Neutrality

The crown is not worn to be seen—it is felt through your field.

To be crowned is not to be above others.
It is to be anchored so deeply within your own center
that nothing outside you can steal your alignment.

The true crown does not shout.
It does not defend.
It does not react.

It emanates.

The crown is authority.
But not the kind the world recognizes.

It is not louder, harsher, or more certain.
It is not made of control.

True authority is the power to remain rooted in alignment
when everything around you pulls toward distortion.

It is the ability to hold clarity
in the presence of confusion—
and not be pulled in.

It is the energetic sovereignty to choose
without justifying, pleasing, or proving.

The Crown as Clarity

When you are crowned, your **yes** is clean.
Your **no** is clear.

Your decisions are not reactions—
they are movements of alignment.

You no longer outsource your truth.
You no longer wait for the world to approve your vision.
You know what is true by how it lives in your field.

Your clarity becomes a blessing to others:
it settles uncertainty, cuts through noise, anchors truth.

The Crown as Divine Neutrality

To wear the crown is to become a neutral field.

Neutral does not mean passive.
Neutral means clear.
Unhooked.
Unattached to needing to control or convince.

The crowned being can listen without absorbing.
Witness without collapsing.
Speak without entangling.

This neutrality is not cold—it is sacred stillness.
It is what makes your presence safe, trustworthy, magnetic.

You do not push.
You radiate.

You do not argue.
You embody.

In a world addicted to reaction,
the crowned one becomes a point of stillness—
and in that stillness, truth is revealed.

How the Crown Appears in Daily Life

You are wearing the crown when:

- You speak with calm certainty, even when challenged

- You walk away without collapse or rage

- You listen to others without abandoning your knowing

- You say yes or no from alignment—not fear or performance

- You choose clarity over control

- You move slowly enough to hear what is true

The crown is not a status.
It is a **frequency**—
and it must be chosen moment by moment.

Every time you return to alignment instead of reaction,
you polish it.
Every time you choose clarity over chaos,
you wear it more fully.
Every time you lead with neutrality instead of need,
your field becomes a throne.

This is the crown of Horus:
Not inherited.
Embodied.

Not imposed.
Transmitted.

Not performed.
Felt.

Walking as the Law Instead of Following It

When your life becomes the temple, there are no steps—only presence.

The highest form of spiritual maturity is not to know many truths—
but to **walk as one.**

The initiate who reaches this point no longer needs to remember every principle in order.
They are no longer asking:

"What should I do now?"

They are asking:

"What is most aligned?"
"What would coherence look like in this moment?"
"What would truth do?"

Because the law is no longer written only in books.
It is written in the way they choose to live.

Walking as the law means your presence teaches.
Your field instructs.
Your life calibrates others simply by existing in alignment.

This does not mean perfection.
It means coherence.

You will still fall out of alignment at times.
But the crowned soul **returns quickly—**
not with guilt, but with clarity.

They no longer need to punish themselves for forgetting.
They simply remember—
and re-align.

Practical Signs You Are Walking as the Law

You are walking as the law when:

- You hold your boundaries without drama or apology

- You speak clearly and simply, from truth not tension

- You pause before action and listen for alignment

- You correct course without shame

- You no longer ask for permission to embody what you already know

- You choose environments, people, and paths that reflect your current frequency—not your past pain

You stop trying to explain yourself to everyone.
You stop fearing disapproval.
You stop rushing to rescue or convince.

Not because you don't care—
but because you care more about coherence than control.

This is divine maturity.

You are not here to memorize rules.
You are here to **become a law of clarity in a disordered world.**

And if you forget?

You don't fall.
You **re-enter**.

You touch your crown.
You breathe.
You speak truth again.
You walk forward.

This is not an act.
It is a return to who you have always been.

To walk as the law is not to shout it.
It is to live it quietly, faithfully, beautifully.

It is to be the flame others gather around—
not because you tell them who to be,
but because you remind them of who they are.

Ritual: Daily Crowning

You no longer seek the law. You wear it.

Purpose:

To return to your sovereign center each day—
not by force, but by remembrance.

To speak and feel the truth:

I do not follow the crown. I walk as it.

This is not a ritual of asking.
It is a ritual of confirmation.

You are not calling in something outside you.
You are sealing what already lives within.

Why This Gesture and Mantra Matter

You have walked the full path.
You have learned to see, balance, speak, surrender, rise, and transmute.

Now, you do not need more.
You need only to return to what you already are—
again and again,
with intention, clarity, and simplicity.

This gesture and mantra are not about power.
They are about **placement**.

They tell the body, the field, the breath:

"Remember.
Return.
Rise."

Even the most sovereign soul forgets.
This ritual ensures you always know how to come back.

You Will Need:

- A moment of stillness

- A place where you can stand or sit upright

- A willingness to affirm your embodiment of truth

---

1. Prepare the Seat

Stand or sit upright.
Let your spine lengthen.
Let your breath slow.
Feel your body aligned and dignified—not stiff, but awake.

You are not calling something down.
You are **making room** for what is already seated in you.

---

2. Speak the Mantra

Inhale deeply.
On the exhale, speak aloud or inwardly:

"I walk crowned."

Feel it not as a hope—
but as a statement of truth.

Let the words calibrate your posture.
Let your energy rise to meet them.

---

3. Activate the Gesture: Form the Crown

Lift your hands slowly to the top of your head.
Fingertips lightly touch, forming a circle.
Pause here.

This is your coronation.
Not given by another—chosen by you.

Feel the ring of your fingers as the symbol of your own sacred alignment.

Breathe into this position.
Let the stillness speak.

---

4. Seal the Field

Lower your hands slowly.
Feel how the air around you has changed.
You are not the same as you were a moment ago.

You are seated again in your rightful place.

The crown is not decoration.
It is structure.
It is frequency.
It is you, remembered.

When to Use This

Use this daily—or anytime you:

- Feel pulled into fear, people-pleasing, or self-doubt

- Are about to speak, lead, decide, or step into visibility

- Want to return to your center before taking aligned action

- Simply wish to remember what you already are

The more you use it—with intention—the more naturally your field carries the crown without needing the gesture.

But even kings and queens rehearse their return.

You have walked through every flame.
You have crossed every gate.
You have seen the hidden laws—
and now, they move through you.

You do not need to become sovereign.

You already are.

Embodiment Key

The Crowned Self (Horus Principle)

Mantra

"I walk crowned."

This is not a wish.
It is a remembrance.

Use this mantra:

- When you feel small, unclear, or misaligned

- Before speaking, deciding, or leading

- Anytime you wish to return to the throne within

Let the words stabilize your frequency.
Let them remind your field:
you are not becoming sovereign—
you are already seated.

Gesture

The Forming of the Crown

With spine upright and breath steady,
lift your hands to the top of your head.
Touch fingertips lightly, forming a ring.

This is not performance.
It is confirmation.

You do not place the crown to gain power.
You place it to **align with what is already yours**.

Use this gesture:

- Before speaking, teaching, or stepping into visibility

- When you feel unseen, unsteady, or disconnected from your truth

- After moments of emotional collapse or energetic leaking

- When returning to your seat of inner leadership

- As a sacred beginning to each day—or whenever you choose to lead as light

---

Anchor Use

Gesture + Mantra as Daily Return to Sovereignty

In any moment of contraction, hesitation, or distortion:

1. Pause.

2. Inhale deeply.

3. Lift your hands and form the crown above your head.

4. As you exhale, speak aloud or inwardly:

"I walk crowned."

Stand or sit in that stillness for a moment.
Let the energy settle.
Let clarity rise.

You have not added anything.
You have simply **remembered what cannot be taken.**

Living Reminder:
The crown is not a reward.
It is the shape of a soul who has chosen coherence over chaos—
again and again.

Thus, the initiate of the Ninth Gate does not need to speak of the path they've walked.

They only need to stand in silence.
The field speaks for them.

They walk not in search—
but as the law itself.

They walk crowned.

Final Blessing

For the One Who Has Remembered

You have walked the nine gates.
You have seen with both eyes.
You have balanced the scales.
You have spoken with living word.
You have read the mirror.
You have bowed before the veil.
You have flowed, burned, risen, and stood.

You are not who you were when you opened this book.
You are not who you will become when you close it.
You are the one who walks now with the flame within.

Let the world forget what it will.
Let time conceal what it must.

But let this be known:

You are the law,
not the seeker of it.

You are the crown,
not the one waiting to wear it.

You are the principle,
in motion, in form, in field.

Walk with quiet knowing.
Speak only what is whole.
Lead without force.

Love with power.
Return to the ritual when needed—
but never forget:

You have already become the temple.

Walk crowned.
Walk true.
Walk as the one who remembers.

Final Words: A Thank You

To you who walked this path—

Thank you.

Thank you for choosing depth in a world that often rewards the surface.
For sitting with silence when noise was easier.
For remembering what so many have forgotten.
And for letting this book not just pass through your hands—
but pass through your being.

These words were never meant to entertain you.
They were meant to awaken something ancient in you.
And you said yes.

I do not know your name,
but I have felt your presence in every page.
This work is alive because you let it become alive in you.

So thank you—
for honoring what is sacred,
for carrying it forward,
and for walking as one who remembers.

From my soul to yours—
in silence, in sovereignty, in flame—

Thank you.

www.ingramcontent.com/pod-product-compliance
Lightning Source LLC
Chambersburg PA
CBHW062108080426
42734CB00012B/2795